The Father's Recipe for Personal Finance
A Believer's Guide

Antoine C. Boyd

King Suite Publications

The names, characters, businesses, places, events and incidents are either the products of the author's imagination or used in a fictional manner. Any resemblance to actual persons, living or dead, or actual events is purely coincidental.

This publication is designed to provide accurate, educational and inspirational information on the subject matter covered. The author is sharing the thought process found useful to him in helping reach his desired level of financial success. If tax, accounting or other professional advice is required, the services of a licensed professional should be enlisted.

ISBN: 0692865292
ISBN-13: 978-0692865293 (King Suite Publications)

Author Contact: thefathersrecipe@gmail.com

DEDICATION

This book is dedicated to the Heavenly Father and all of His true believers regardless of denomination, residence, or anything else used to separate our union with one another. To family, friends, neighbors, co-workers, classmates, and even doubters who contributed to my growth... salute.

TABLE OF CONTENTS

ACKNOWLEDGMENTS

To my mom for raising me and always being someone to depend on
regardless of the predicament.

To my paternal great aunt/grandmother for all of the unconditional love
while we were on this earth together and my maternal grandmother for
making sure the Spirit flowed throughout our family.

To CJ for challenging me to live outside my calculated box.

To my brothers, sisters, cousins, and close friends for any part you've
played in my life throughout this journey.

To the Pastor of ABLF Church for making sure the pure and unadulterated
Word is brought forth.

And to my Lord and Savior Jesus Christ.

PREFACE

The study of God's Word and Finance are two things I'm very passionate about. I believe the Heavenly Father provides a blueprint on how we can be most effective in our day to day living. Managing money happens to be something that impacts almost every one of us in some capacity. That's why I took a journey to link what God says about the topic in hopes to better my financial situation and possibly help others. My goal was to write in a manner that would be consistent with believers in general. If someone is Christian as I am, Jewish, or Muslim for instance, these principles should still be applicable to them and their families. I can attest firsthand that after applying them to my life, my situation started to turn around in less than a year and continues to get better in a number of ways.

The story is told of a father giving advice to his two adolescent children while they are preparing a family meal. They have a phenomenal new recipe to try as well as a deep conversation about personal finance. The father answers several questions either the children or people they know have regarding money management, retirement plans, debt, and a few other things that are relevant to the subject. He explains it in a very basic way so that any teenager or adult should be able to grasp. His hope is that these principles can be passed down from generation to generation in order for his family to always be well positioned economically.

Growing up in an east Baltimore housing projects, I didn't have anyone who really took the time to break down these lessons for me at an early age. There were questions and situations that I saw impacting my family financially but no one seemed to teach best practices in my neighborhood. We weren't surrounded by Wall Street managers, accountants, or financial planners. But we still needed to know how to manage money. And of course everyone was interested. As I got older, experienced a few challenges of my own, and finally gave God my attention, He cleared my mind enough to show me my true passion. I never knew I loved the subject of financial management although I was well aware that I liked to spend money. I started looking at television shows that discussed money matters and took pleasure in learning about the stock market. I also switched my career from IT to Finance within a former company and really started to enjoy coming to work regularly. I decided to go back to college and change my major after a nine year layoff in order to pursue a

Bachelor of Science degree in Finance. Navigating through the courses I learned that even then, most of my classes primarily focused on big business and corporate financial management. I still wanted to concentrate on relevant topics that impacted me daily. Where was the information about how to get out of debt, what is the company referring to when they say 401k or 403b plan, or why is a budget so important? I also wanted to know how God felt about all of this. If His Word was a blueprint on how to live, shouldn't I be able to find the answer to these questions that impact my life or family life regularly?

In my research and study of comparing textbook knowledge to the Word, I believe to have found several principles that work for every believer irrespective of their denomination. I've always wondered why if Christians, Jews, and Muslims believed in the same God of Abraham for example, shouldn't most of the life principles each of them practice overlap? I've concluded that they actually do in a number of ways, especially in the subject of money. This book will provide a guide on being successful financially whether you're a believer earning a million dollars each year or minimum wage. Parents who want to learn about relevant financial issues that have a daily impact and be able to pass down knowledge to their offspring would also find this story very beneficial. I would personally like to thank everyone who gave me a chance to help them manage their funds, my employers who provided an opportunity to work in financial management at an organization, my loved ones, and most importantly God Almighty, my true Inspiration and Teacher.

INTRO: GROCERY SHOPPING

We'll have to meet about that tomorrow to discuss more of the details. I'm a bit skeptical especially when there's that much money involved. But let me go now. I'm at the school picking up my kids. I'll see you in the office around 9 am.

Ok.

Bye.

Hey AJ, how's it going buddy?

"I'm good" AJ answered. "Just a little hungry."

Well we're heading to the grocery store right after we pull off. Where's your sister?

"She was right behind me but had to run back to get her jacket."

"There she is coming down the steps now" AJ said to his dad as he pointed.

"Hi daddy" Zoe greeted with a big smile on her face.

Hey baby. How was school?

"It was exhausting" Zoe replied after buckling in her seatbelt. "I had two quizzes and a presentation."

Well I'm sure you did well.

"I believe so. We find out next Friday."

I can't wait to hear about it.

"Where are we headed?" Zoe asked.

"We're on our way to the grocery store" AJ said.

"Good. I need some more frozen pizza. I noticed my last one must have been eaten by the Tooth fairy" Zoe stated as she looked at her brother with a side eye and her lips poked out.

"Don't look at me" AJ said grinning from ear to ear. "The temptation is real sometimes."

It's ok. We'll grab a few more while we are there buying food for dinner tonight. AJ doesn't mind using part of his allowance to replace your pizza.

"Huh" AJ said surprised with his mouth wide open.

"I couldn't agree more" Zoe replied smiling at her brother.

"What are we making dad?" Zoe asked.

I think we should try this recipe I read in a book for some Salmon with a Balsamic glaze.

"Mmmmm. That sounds yummy." Zoe replied imagining the taste.

"Well let's hurry up so we can get started" AJ said as they pulled into the parking spot.

"Hi. Would you all be interested in buying some Girl Scout cookies" said a young girl with freckles standing in the parking lot.

Absolutely. I'll purchase three packs for me and my kids. You can keep the change.

"Thank you very much for the support" said the young girl as she handed over the three packs.

"Thanks dad. I love these" Zoe said.

"Yes they are really good" AJ chimed in.

Well you two can split my pack but don't eat them until after dinner. I like to buy them just for the support. Stand here for a second while I go grab the cart.

"So what do we need?" Zoe asked as they started walking through the aisles.

Just a few things we didn't have at the house. Let me grab my list so we can get going before the checkout line becomes full.

"Good afternoon" said the cashier as she scanned the groceries. "Is this all of the items?"

I believe that's it.

"Ok great. Your total is on the screen" the cashier replied.

I'm sorry I forgot to give you these coupons. Is it too late?

"No problem. I can take them" the cashier said as she reached out her hand.

Thanks.

"Here's your new total."

"That saved a few bucks" Zoe added.

It sure did. I love looking for coupons before I go shopping. Lowering expenses is almost as good as earning more income.

"I'm a fan of deals and sales myself" AJ chimed in.

"I like to look online for coupon codes before I shop. There are a few sites that have numerous ones for people to try" Zoe said.

"I know. Some of them don't work however" AJ added. "But I still sit there and try a few just to make sure."

I think it's worth trying. You're not losing anything by making the attempt.

"A penny saved is a penny earned" Zoe responded as she hears her father saying this from time to time.

You know that's my motto.

"Hi Mr. Hart" Zoe and AJ said waving at one of the neighbors.

"Hiiii my favorite family" Mr. Hart replied. "Out grocery shopping again?"

"Yes sir" AJ replied. "We're making some Salmon with balsamic sauce smothered all over it" Zoe said salivating.

"Ooooh tasty." Mr. Hart replied. "Maybe I can bring over some of my famous beef franks and beans to add to the feast" Mr. Hart said before bursting out with a big laugh.

No thanks. But you are more than welcome to come over and get a plate.

"I'm just kidding. I have a lot of work to finish up in the back" Mr. Hart replied declining the invitation.

"What are you building now? An amusement park" AJ teased knowing Mr. Hart loves to build and has the best back yard in the neighborhood.

"Oh just a little something I've been thinking about" Mr. Hart replied. "But now that you said amusement park, I have some other ideas I need to go write down."

We'll be over tomorrow to check it all out.

"Bye Mr. Hart. See you tomorrow" Zoe said waving goodbye.

Ok guys. Let's unload the bags, wash our hands, and get busy.

CHAPTER I: GOD 1ST

Zoe, turn the oven to 400 degrees while I line the baking sheet with aluminum foil. AJ you can grab the cooking spray.

"Hey dad. How does Mr. Hart pay for all of those things he builds in his back yard?" AJ asked as he reached towards the top shelf to grab the spray.

"I've been thinking about that as well" Zoe added. "He must be rich."

Well we're all rich as believers.

"I know we're blessed but he must be blessed with a ton of cash" AJ said while handing his dad the spray.

He's definitely blessed but not with a ton of cash. Or at least he's never mentioned it to me. He's just very smart with managing the cash he does have.

"Just like I'll be when I get my Finance degree like you dad" Zoe said.

You still want to major in Finance next year.

"Yes" Zoe replied. "I have to know how to handle the cash so I can get my big house with a huuuge garden, a kitchen with an island, and a Jacuzzi in my master bedroom" Zoe said shaking her head up and down with her eyes closed.

"When my clothing line takes off I'll be able to get a mansion to park my future Rolls-Royce" AJ said rubbing his hands together.

So I see you are still focused on being an entrepreneur.

"Yes sir" AJ replied shaking his head in a yes motion.

That's good. Are you both not content with the things you have already?

"I am for sure but just like to dream a little" Zoe responded.

"I'm happy with what we've got but why not shoot for the stars?" AJ said.

I agree. We are humble believers but if we can be blessed with those things, I don't see a problem with it as long as we follow the Father's blueprint. And if He blesses us with more, no one will be able to take it away.

"True. So what do you mean by the Father's blueprint?" Zoe asked.

There are principles given about finance and money management in order to help us live prosperously. The first step as we all know in this household is to keep God first. We are supposed to seek Him in prayer and educate ourselves about how He wants us to live our lives. And part of living is handling money wisely. See God gives knowledge and understanding to the believers that strive for it. Being wise and making good choices will help you build those houses. You'll be able to purchase some of those things you're dreaming about over time. But you cannot allow it to be your motivating factor. Living a better life as each week goes by is our motivation. Then some of those blessings if not all will follow. You understand?

"Yes" Zoe replied while AJ nodded his head in agreement.

We have one Master in this household. We stick within His guidelines first and foremost. School and others may teach you one thing about money but if it doesn't agree with the Father's lessons, we follow the Father. Most of the time it probably will if it's sound advice. We just have to learn how to relate the two. But when they don't agree, we cannot serve God while going against what He says to do. We follow His finance plan or we may end up in some bad situations.

"Like some of the evil ones we saw on that television series with the financiers swindling their clients?" Zoe asked.

Yes. That federal jail time is just not worth it.

"Is money really the root of evil as everyone likes to say?" AJ asked.

I don't think so. Money is just a tool used to trade or buy things. It doesn't do any harm by itself. To prove my point, I'm going to lay this ten dollar bill on the table while we finish cooking and we'll see if it does anything good or bad.

"Of course it won't" Zoe said smiling.

"It may crawl into my pocket at some point but that's probably about it" AJ said before chuckling.

I'm sure that will be with you lending a helping hand. But by itself, it'll just remain there. So it's not money but what we do with and for that money which can cause good or bad things to occur. If we fall in love with acquiring money and it makes us hurt others or act arrogantly, that is when we're in the wrong. That's not how the

Father wants us to conduct ourselves. And remember He's first. So I encourage you two to seek earning it as long as your attempts are within His guidelines foremost and then the law. Got it?

"Yes" AJ and Zoe both replied.

"Dad, do you think God wants His people to be rich?" AJ asked.

"I think He does" Zoe replied before her father could respond. "I don't see why He would want us to be poor."

Well that's a good point Zoe. I'm not sure He has plans for everyone to be millionaires however. I do believe He wants his people to flourish and even have a little overflow to help others. And how can we help others or raise families if we do not have anything more than just our own basic necessities?

"That's true" AJ replied.

He even gives permission to test Him when it comes to having more than enough.

"I thought we were never supposed to test God?" Zoe asked as she was becoming confused.

You are correct except when He gives permission to do so. He says to test Him by preserving His house of worship with whatever it needs and see if He'll pour out a major blessing. So much that it overflows into the lives of those connected to you. Imagine if we put a cup on that counter and start pouring from our big water pitcher. What will ultimately happen if we keep pouring?

"The water will overflow and wet the counter" Zoe responded.

"The placemat, bottom of the mixer, and everything else near it would eventually get wet as well" AJ added.

Exactly. Everything connected to the cup would soon be wet with that same water. That's the type of blessing I envision the Father speaking about when He says to try Him by obeying His commands. If we follow His way of living and manage our money within His guidelines, others close to us will also benefit.

"Right. We may be able to buy them something or help them with an issue" AJ said as he started to understand his father.

That's why I personally believe God wants each one of His followers to be prosperous. So it's alright to seek becoming wealthy. Just remember that the more we have, the more we'll be required to help others.

"Makes sense to me" AJ replied.

"Me too. With that being said... can you overflow some of your money into my account for the mall tomorrow please?" Zoe added with a big smile on her face.

You always find an opportunity, don't you? I'll see what I can do.

CHAPTER II: FIRST FRUITS

AJ grab that small saucepan from the bottom cabinet and put some cooking spray on it. Zoe you can stir the cloves of garlic for a few minutes until they get soft.

"Ok" Zoe replied.

Now keeping God first also means giving Him your first before you start to do everything else with your money. That's partially how we get to that overflow.

"Is that why you always tell us to save ten percent of what we get for God and another ten for ourselves?" AJ asked.

Yes indeed. It is much easier to give when you don't already have plans to spend your entire paycheck for example. You should only plan to spend the remainder after taking out those portions and calculating what's leftover. It's much harder to make yourself give when you already have the money allocated to something else.

"That first ten percent is the tithe, right dad?" Zoe asked.

It is. Tithe literally means tenth. We are to take our first fruits or whatever we earn and put that away for God. Back in the old day's some people took the first of their flocks or something they grew such as different types of fruit in order to give a tenth. Presently, it's more common to give ten percent of your income. Especially in the U.S.

"So if I make $10 an hour over 40 hours per week which equals $400, am I supposed to save $40 for God first and then another $40 to put into my Savings account?" AJ asked.

Not exactly. You didn't really receive $400 due to taxes and other deductions you may have. Look at it in terms of what you received in your actual account. That is called take home pay or net payment.

"Ok. So I just take the percentages from what actually goes into my bank account from the job" AJ said.

Right. You can also tithe any other income you get including tax refunds since the tax withholding was never tithed. That way you capture everything as you receive it, giving God your first fruits before you start spending.

"Dad, I've been meaning to ask you. Why does God need money?" Zoe asked looking a bit puzzled.

It's not that He needs it or wants to go buy things. He already owns everything and can create anything. What He did in my opinion is used the tithing principle to keep the Word flowing. The tithes are brought into the storehouses so that the storehouse and its ministers can continue spreading His Word. It takes money to maintain a building, print flyers, buy materials, pay utilities, etc. Some storehouses also become very large to a point where staff is needed to sustain the ministry. That will have associated costs as well.

"Right because the staff won't all be volunteers like us" AJ added.

This is true. Most of them would probably be more willing to volunteer a lot of time if they could. But because they have a family and bills to take care of, keeping a job with a regular paycheck or sustaining their own profitable business is necessary for survival. We live in a society where money is used almost daily and jobs can really decrease your free time.

"Dad, can we tithe to that charity down the street where we volunteer?" AJ asked.

Not really. We can start donating a few additional dollars when we have it but the storehouses God is referring to are the ones that specifically spread the Word. Donations to charities are just that. Charitable contributions. Although they are very important as well.

"That makes sense. Maybe we should explain this to Uncle Cory. He said the only tithe he gives is to the homeless because his pastor drives a fancy car while he can barely buy a kid's meal if it's not pay day" AJ said before they all burst into laughter.

Your Uncle Cory does not give anything to anybody. That's his excuse for not tithing. I've told him before just because he believes a pastor mismanages the money doesn't make God's Word change. If he feels so strongly about his pastor not doing right with the tithes, he can just go to another house of worship. Don't ignore God's Word because of something a man maybe or maybe not have done. Furthermore, the pastor he is specifically referring to is really a great person and I doubt whole heartedly if he's mishandling funds. He does drive a nice car but he also writes books, has a vending machine business, and contracts as a medical coder. Trust me, that's nothing more than your Uncle Cory making excuses for not giving.

"If he set aside tithing and saving before he spent any of his paycheck, it would be easier" Zoe said.

I tried telling him that for many years. When you get your paycheck, remove the tithe and savings portion before planning to spend a dime. It works like a charm.

"What if he has too many expenses for that at this point?" AJ asked. "Maybe more than 90% of his paycheck is used to pay bills."

Then he should trust that God is understanding and pray that the Heavenly Father blesses the little he can give until he has enough to tithe the full ten percent. I believe if he shows how faithful he is over the few things; it won't be too long before he starts getting much more. Especially if he matures spiritually along the way.

"One of my classmates said his father told him that Jesus got rid of tithing. Is that true?" AJ asked while looking up towards the ceiling trying to recall the exact conversation.

It's not true based upon my reading. I've researched that argument specifically and found where He called some people hypocrites for paying tithes without exercising the more important matters such as judgment, mercy, and faith. The people He was speaking to were meticulous tithers. He then clearly told them they should continue tithing, while also being just and merciful. Never did He say to stop tithing.

"My teammate said her father used to give $20 each Sunday until he found out what type of car the First Lady was driving. He then reduced it to $10" Zoe said before they shared a quick laugh.

You know what; I'm starting to think both of your friend's fathers may be associates of your Uncle Cory.

CHAPTER III: PLANTING GOOD SEEDS

Zoe please mix up the honey, balsamic vinegar, mustard, and the salt and pepper.

"Ok dad. How much?" Zoe asked.

You'll need a tablespoon of honey, four teaspoons of the Dijon mustard, and about a third cup of the balsamic vinegar. I'll grab the white wine from the fridge so we can add a tablespoon of that as well.

"This is going to be good" Zoe said.

"I can't wait to eat" AJ added. "How long does it have to cook?"

About 20 minutes after we are done prepping. Just a few more steps.

"It takes a lot to make it this tasty" Zoe added.

It does. It takes hard work and investment to really get the best results. The same with our financial lives.

"I know exactly what you mean" AJ said thinking about his community service job from last summer. "When I worked at the center, I had to mop the floors, clean the bathroom, wipe down the mirrors, and clean the glass on every door in the building. And at the end of the night, I even had to take out the trash from each room." AJ explained as he wiped his brow.

"They were preparing you for your career if you don't keep them grades up" Zoe said before she and her father started laughing.

There's nothing wrong with that type of career or anything that's honest, legal, and someone is willing to pay for.

"I'm going to work very hard when I get into my career" Zoe said.

I know you will because you do so now. While in school, you have to work hard in order to get good grades which can then lead to scholarships for college. That'll save us a ton especially if you get enough for a full ride. Then after you work hard in college and graduate, you'll have more career opportunities and possibly generate a lot more income. All of this being a result of planting good seeds of hard work while young and in school. Reaping later what you sowed earlier.

"I've been working hard on my clothing line. Reading everything you've recommended Dad. I'm almost at the point where I can put a draft of the business plan together for you to review. I've been on it non-stop" AJ added.

That's good. Just remember not to overwork yourself. Even if it's all mental, you must have a break built-in. Hard work is encouraged but not 24/7. You have to have at least one rest day. That's why my business phone gets turned off by 11:59 pm on Friday night and doesn't get turned back on until Sunday evening at the earliest. Some weekend's I have to put in a little work but definitely not both days. At least one day is for rest and the Word.

"Hey Dad. What about people who can't work? Like the guy we saw in the clinic using a wheelchair?" AJ asked remembering someone he likes to help whenever he sees him at doctor appointments.

That's a little different. God is kind and understanding. If someone is disabled and has too many challenges preventing them from being able to work, they don't have the same expectations as we do. God sometimes gives extra money or a genuine passion for people like that and we are required to assist them as we pass along. Just like you love to help him whenever you both are at the clinic. I believe that's the Father's design.

"Yes I really do. He is so hilarious with his old war stories" AJ said smiling and shaking his head thinking about the last time they spoke.

"There are some disabled people that work. We have an assistant in the counselor's office who sits in a wheelchair" Zoe mentioned.

There are a lot of disabled individuals who are employed. If they're able to make it, that's great. Just make sure you help them if you are ever nearby and they look like they need assistance. Don't be overbearing however. Some like to feel more independent. But you can at least offer.

"It must be hard getting around like that all day. Especially in a manual wheelchair" AJ said.

I'm sure it is. They show a ton of ambition and perseverance just putting forth the effort in my opinion. Unlike people who are perfectly able bodied and no intellectual disabilities but sit around all day doing nothing. For people like that who won't work, I'm not sure how they plan to generate any wealth for themselves and their families. It's no one else's fault but your own when you don't give a legitimate effort.

"I agree" Zoe said nodding her head.

Never be lazy. Always work hard for what you want and make sure it's within God's boundaries. The results are better that way.

"You hear that sis? When my business takes off from all of this hard work, I might let you drive one of my cars on the weekend" AJ said jokingly to Zoe.

"Boy bye" Zoe quickly replied. "You better hope I let you pick from my garden when your little girlfriends run away with the money."

You two need a sitcom.

CHAPTER IV: BASICS OF BUDGETING

Now we have to let this simmer for a few minutes.

"Here's the top dad" Zoe said reaching her arm over.

No need for that right now. We'll watch it simmer uncovered until it starts getting thick.

"Ok" Zoe responded putting the top back down.

"Something must be malfunctioning with this" AJ said looking down at his cell phone.

"Why do you say that?" Zoe asked as she walked over to look.

"My phone company just texted me the bill for last month" AJ said looking puzzled. "It's higher than normal and I have unlimited minutes."

"You better go check your statement" Zoe suggested. "It's probably from all of those in-app purchases you make in your poor attempt to keep up with me in the game" Zoe said smiling at her brother.

"You know what... those 99 cents here and there really does add up" AJ said shaking his head upset with himself.

"Hopefully I didn't hurt your budget too much leaving you in the dust" Zoe said before chuckling.

"Whatever" AJ replied. "I don't need to budget for that."

You need to budget for everything son.

"Even in-app purchases?" AJ asked.

Does it cost money?

"Well yes. But not that much" AJ replied.

It doesn't matter how much. The first step in knowing how well you are doing financially is creating a budget. You have to know your income versus the expenses you have.

"That's the only way to tell if you overspend" Zoe added.

That's right. I've developed budgets for clients who had no idea they were operating at a loss every month. They spent more than they brought in. And do you know why they never knew?

"No budget, huh?" AJ said smiling.

Correct. Some of them were losing small sums of cash over time which eventually added up to a big problem. After a few months they started to realize they didn't have enough money for basic household items. And a few others came to the realization when they didn't have enough funds to take a trip with friends or make a big purchase.

"So how did they go that long without running out of money?" AJ asked.

Some of them participate in the good old robbing Peter to pay Paul.

"I've heard Uncle Cory say that but never asked him what he meant by it" Zoe said fully attentive to finally hear the meaning behind the saying.

I'm sure he's mastered that skill set. But what it means is that he skips one bill this month to pay another one. Then the next month he may skip the vendor he just paid to pay one that's more delinquent. Just continuing to juggle and hoping for something like a tax refund or for me to give another loan he probably won't pay back.

"Or hit the lottery" AJ added before snickering.

Those are not ways I recommend to you two with regards to paying bills. Make sure you always keep track of your income from work and your allowance. Then check your expenses to see if you can cover all of them.

"What if I don't have enough to pay all of my bills?" AJ asked.

At that point you determine which bills are absolutely necessary and try figuring out how to reduce the rest. Some of the luxuries may have to go such as that cell phone or at least the games which aren't free. But if you followed what I always teach with taking out the tithe and ten percent savings before planning to spend a dime, you shouldn't have too many issues with overspending. You've already budgeted the money to some extent. You just have to make a complete budget to cover everything else and to help remember what expenses you currently have before adding a new one. Another reason why a budget is so important is it shows how much extra you have left over after all expenses. That's the amount you can use to donate, buy something new, save for a trip, in-app purchases, etc. Without a budget you won't truly know if you have the ability to do any of those things.

"That makes sense" AJ said.

Businesses need budgets as well.

"I am sure they do with all of the expenses and employee salaries" Zoe added.

This is true. Cash is the bloodline of business. If you don't manage it properly, you may not have a business for much longer.

"So dad. What do you tell your clients when they decide to create a personal budget?" AJ asked.

I always advise each one of them the same exact way. They need to first write down whatever income is receive regularly such as from a job, investments, or anything else that can be counted on consistently. Then they have to note every penny spent each day for about a month or two. That includes buying gas for their car, eating out, a cup of coffee, a stick of bubble gum, whatever. Anything they spend money on needs to be written down. My goal is for them to become very familiar with their spending habits and to constantly keep their budget template updated. Even though we start with an initial budget and a plan to get out of any financial problems they may have, I reiterate that this is something which will need to be reviewed and adjusted for the rest of their lives. Whether they are still working with me or not.

"That gets me to thinking" Zoe said. "I'll have to examine my budget after this weekend. I'm sure there are a few items I may have forgotten to include."

Why not today?

"Because I have to get my nails done and that's not up for debate" Zoe said shaking her head no from side to side.

Every penny counts so this needs to be on your budget going forward. How much do you have to pay for your nails?

"Well if I go to the place I really like, I pay about $30" Zoe replied while looking down at the back of her hands.

"I can do them for half the price and help you save a few bucks" AJ suggested with a big smile on his face.

"No thanks. I would go into debt before that were to happen" Zoe quickly replied shaking her head.

"You hear that dad?" AJ replied. "She would rather be in debt instead of letting her brother paint her nails. And that's your little finance lady."

I don't know son. I may have to co-sign that decision.

CHAPTER V: BE MORE CAREFUL WITH DEBT

AJ, grab the baking sheet and place the six pieces of salmon on it. Please leave a little space between each one.

"Ok" AJ replied before arranging the five ounce fillets.

"Dad. Can I borrow five dollars please?" AJ asked.

Why do you need it?

"I have to repay one of my classmates who lent it to me when we were at the game on Wednesday night" AJ replied.

Ok. Did he charge you an interest rate?

"I would have charged you at least 25% so luckily you didn't ask me" Zoe said smiling.

"No he didn't because he's on my real friend and family list" AJ responded while looking at his sister.

"I'd be buried in debt borrowing from you" AJ added.

"You sure would. Or you could complete my chores for a dollar an hour until it's all paid back" Zoe teased with the biggest smirk on her face.

Well she has a point son. It is written that a borrower is the servant to the lender. In addition to making the decision on how much you'll get paid, that 25% interest rate would be the toughest part of the deal. Interest is a capital killer so to speak. When people go to the store and put a television on a credit card for example, they end up spending much more for the product.

"Right because the interest added to the price" Zoe replied.

Exactly. So if the regular price for that big screen is discounted and someone buys it with financing or a credit card, they could quite possibly end up losing the full discount after paying the interest.

"I'm not sure why they would do that for a television" AJ said as he started to understand how the discount would be completely gone with this type of arrangement.

Trust me. Some do it for a lot more than just a TV. It's primarily because they want something now and don't think about the full cost including interest. Some people also feel like the reduced price will never be the same or this will be the last day to ever receive a sale. I've been living on this earth for quite a few years and those sales prices have come and gone as long as I've been alive. If it's not a necessity, it's better to save and then make the purchase.

"True" AJ replied as his sister nodded in agreement.

Ok AJ. Brush some of that balsamic glaze on the salmon and pass it to Zoe to sprinkle it with the oregano.

"Let me ask this question. What about buying something like a car or a house?" Zoe asked as she added the seasoning. "That may take a very long time in order to save enough to pay the full price."

Point well taken. As far as a car, it's ok to finance if it's needed for your family or used to earn money such as commuting to and from work. It would be great to buy it with cash but if not, I'll accept a little financing. Just make sure it's something you can afford. What I don't want to see is you buying a luxury vehicle and financing it for six years or so. If it takes that long to pay off, you probably can't truly afford that specific automobile.

"Do most people have a five year loan?" AJ asked as he remembered something he read on the internet.

Perhaps. But personally I never took a five year loan for either of those vehicles. Three years was always my max. If I couldn't afford to pay it off in three years after applying my down payment, it was beyond my budget.

"Why three?" Zoe asked.

It's just a personal calculation I came up with for myself. I wanted to pay it off as soon as possible and then have it for several years afterwards with no car payment. That's what I did for the black car in the garage. After it was paid off, I then saved that payment amount for a couple of years and put it towards paying for our family van which was fully purchased right before the term was up. Now both of them are paid off within a collective six year period.

"Two for the term of one. That sounds smart" Zoe said while nodding her head smiling.

It works. The house on the other hand is not as easy. The cost is much more.

"Do you have a similar rule for buying a house?" AJ asked.

I do but it's a little different. I still make sure it's something I can

afford. Before choosing a home, I always calculate how much of a monthly payment I am able to make without impacting any of my other responsibilities. This includes determining my limit for the principal, interest, taxes, insurance, and even a little extra for routine maintenance. I would then visit my credit union in order to get pre-qualified for a loan. Because I had a good credit score and a nice down payment, they emphasized how I could make a larger purchase than what I calculated for myself. But of course I didn't bite. After that, I would work with my realtor and his team to help me pick something within my predetermined range.

"You stick to your own calculation no matter what, huh?" Zoe asked.

Exactly. Let them calculate what's best for them and we'll calculate what's best for us. I did the same thing before I moved into our old apartment. I didn't have to calculate things such as taxes and interest but I did look at my budget to determine what was affordable for me at the time.

"Did you like living in the apartment more since things like maintenance were included?" AJ asked. "I know you love your back yard and the space but I'm just asking in terms of money."

No. I like having the house and could see us residing here for at least another five years. We were going to have a living expense regardless. Whether it was rent or a mortgage, we had to make some type of payment. But with buying a house, I started building equity in a property.

"What's that?" AJ asked.

It's basically how much of the property's value you own. With an apartment, the property owners have all of the equity. The renters aren't entitled to any of it. With buying the house, every payment earns me more equity as the amount owed decreases until it's paid off completely. Then whatever value it has after that is all mine. If I were to move for example, I could sell the house and keep whatever equity built up. With renting, I would move and only keep my personal belongings.

"So you have more assets" Zoe added.

That is correct my little finance lady. The other benefit about buying the house instead of renting is you get to deduct some of the mortgage interest from your taxable income. That will help to lower your tax bill.

"And get more of a refund?" AJ asked.

There are other factors but in essence, yes.

"So is it better to keep the mortgage loan forever so you can always get a refund when you file?" AJ asked.

Not exactly. Some people share that opinion but personally I do not. Let's look at it this way. When you pay taxes, you're paying a percentage of your earnings based upon your tax bracket. So it's not the case where if you paid $7,000 in interest you'll get that full $7,000 refunded with a deduction. Even if it was, I would prefer not to give it up front only to receive it back interest free. But the way it works is if you're in a 25% bracket, that $7,000 mortgage interest deduction would essentially have the benefit of about $1,750. But remember, you paid $7,000 to a bank in order get that $1,750.

"Ok. That doesn't make much sense" Zoe said looking up in the air as to calculate it herself. "I would have been $5,250 richer if I paid off the loan."

Precisely. It just doesn't make sense if that's the only reason why you wanted to keep the loan. So if you can afford to pay it off while still having an emergency fund, enough to routinely contribute to retirement savings, and no other immediate concerns, pay the house off. But it is undeniably a blessing to have that deduction when you're not in a position to completely pay off the mortgage. I do hope our government continues to keep it in place.

"You also pay much more for the house as we were discussing earlier about financing" AJ added.

Indeed. The longer you make interest payments, the more it adds to the total cost. And people who would be better served with the standard deduction like you two would not take advantage of this tax benefit any way. But that's something we can discuss when we prepare our returns.

"Hey dad. Do businesses work the same way?" AJ asked. "What I mean by that is do I have to wait until I make a lot of money before growing my clothing line?"

Sometimes you may have to take chances and get a loan especially if you have a plan as to how that funding will help your earnings grow. If your business is growing and you need extra cash for something like restocking the inventory… that would be fine.

"Ok. I understand because I need the inventory in order to sell and make money" AJ said.

Correct. You want to keep the business flowing and quickly satisfying your customers' requests.

"One of my teachers mentioned that he had to cosign his brother's loan before he could buy his new car" AJ recalled.

Well I definitely do not want you two cosigning for anyone. It becomes your responsibility just as much as it is the other signer. And if they cannot pay for whatever reason, your credit history will be negatively impacted. I've had several clients learn this the hard way. They had a friend beg them to co-sign for a car and promised to always make the payment. Then at some point before the loan was completely paid off, the friend could no longer pay or just stopped making payments for whatever reason. That ended up causing major financial difficulties as well as a damaged relationship. It's just not worth it. Look at it this way. If a bank who has millions of dollars does not want to take the risk on someone, why would you who have much less sign with that same person? Especially if you can't afford to pay it all on your own. Or what if it is a responsible friend and some unforeseen circumstances happened beyond their control? It's just too risky.

"Did we cosign with you for that credit card?" Zoe asked her father.

No not at all. Because I manage money well, I added you two as authorized users in order to improve your credit scores. I only use the card for the cash back reward points and never for anything I couldn't pay off within the grace period. Groceries, gas, and small items that I already have the cash for are things that may be swiped. If an emergency were to occur and I didn't have enough reserve cash, that would be the only other reason. Outside of that, I use my debit card.

"Ok. I'm still waiting on a copy of that card in the mail" Zoe said with a grin.

Well don't hold your breath while you wait. You're authorized but cannot use it if that makes any sense.

"I've heard Uncle Cory saying he's going to pay this bill and not worry about that one even though they were both passed due" Zoe said. "Isn't he hurting himself by not making payments on all of his delinquent accounts?"

He really is. Especially since he earns a decent salary but chooses to go have fun instead.

"Maybe you should explain this stuff to him and then give some advice on how he can get out of debt" AJ added.

Please don't think I haven't been trying. I even provided a strategy that I think is best for him.

"What's that?" AJ asked.

I informed him that usually paying off the debt with the highest interest rate first is the smartest approach. It saves the most money. However, he will not stick to that plan if he doesn't see any progress or one of them falling off sooner rather than later. So for him he should pay the minimum due monthly on each one. Any extra money can then be used to pay off the smaller balances first. Then once they are paid off, he can take the extra that was being applied and put it to the next smallest balance. Keep doing it that way until they are all addressed. And most importantly, don't add any new debt without it being an absolute emergency. This method will also help to improve his credit score.

"He told me his trip to Jamaica was an emergency one time" Zoe said as they all laughed.

Let me guess, to get away from the bill collectors.

"How did you know?" Zoe said laughing even more.

Your Uncle Cory has been saying that for years.

CHAPTER VI: INVESTING IS IMPORTANT

That's enough glaze for now. Please put the fish in the oven for about 10 minutes or so and then you can brush on the remaining glaze when it's done. Also get the salt and pepper ready.

"Dad did you learn all of these things from school or the real world?" Zoe asked as she shut the oven door. "The textbooks in my classes do not discuss matters that are a part of everyday life. When we discuss Finance, it's usually about businesses or stocks and bonds."

Well I've learned about personal finance from school and real life. Primarily through life experiences however. School provided a strong foundation that I was able to build upon. When you get to college and advance to your major courses, you'll get into the specifics a little more. But it's always been my opinion that personal finance should start in the home and well before college age. God shares with us that good understanding gains favor. It's my responsibility to make sure you both learn from my experiences in order to make better choices in life. Managing money is definitely a skill used on a consistent basis. Always take what you've learned, research it a little more, and add to it if possible. Then share it with the rest of us. Invest in yourself with quality education and in your family.

"I agree dad" AJ said. "I've been reading about investing a lot lately."

Really? That's great. Do you want to share some things you've learned?

"Well one thing I've learned is that stocks aren't as expensive as I thought. I was under the impression that you needed about $10,000 just to buy one" AJ said.

I think a lot of people believe that and it turns them off before they even get started. There are some stocks that have a large per share price while you can get others for much less than $50.

"I was looking at my favorite clothing company and saw their share price was currently less than my new sneakers" AJ said as he nodded in agreement.

"I'm going to look up a few after dinner tonight and see if I can buy a share or two" Zoe said.

Not a bad idea. Let me know which ones you like and we can chat about them together. My only recommendation for people who want to invest is that you start after you have an emergency fund saved and if your debt is being paid off properly as previously discussed.

"How much of an emergency fund should we have?" AJ asked.

It all varies based upon the individual and their situation. Some who have more stable jobs and a great resume could possibly save a bit less. Others who have either unstable jobs or little to no investments to sell if necessary may need to save much more. My rule of thumb would be about six months' worth of expenses.

"Why six months?" AJ asked.

I think that should generally cover the bills long enough for someone to apply for jobs, go through the interview process a few times, wait to hear back that they are hired, and then get at least one or two paychecks. That's just a rough estimate of course.

"That makes sense" AJ replied as he agreed with his father's logic.

Now that emergency fund should be kept in a savings account.

"So we shouldn't invest it even if the market would earn more?" Zoe asked.

No. Try not to invest any of your emergency fund. You need to keep it liquid.

"What is liquid?" AJ asked.

It just means you should be able to convert to cash quickly when needed. With an investment account, you have to sell invested products in order to convert them into cash. Then you would hope they haven't decreased in value at the time of a crisis. The savings account wouldn't require that conversion step. My recommendation would be to take the smaller interest from savings while ensuring your emergency cash is safer. Only invest in the stock market with money you won't need for at least five years.

"Ok. So the bank has to give the money in my savings account back to me no matter what?" AJ asked.

Essentially. Make sure the savings account is at an institution which is FDIC or NCUA insured. So if the bank or credit union were to fail, that coverage would kick in and you can still get your money up to the insured limit. That's what makes it safer. And you want your emergency funds safe as well as easily accessible.

"I can't wait to start investing and making some big money" AJ said rubbing his hands together.

You already are and probably don't know it.

"Why do you say that?" AJ asked as he was puzzled.

Well your summer job is with an organization that allows you to take part in a 401k retirement plan.

"Oh, I remember when we filled out the paper work and picked some of the choices from the introductory packet" AJ said nodding as he recalled.

Right. I should have explained it a little more at that time but that's really the first step most people take as far as getting involved in the market. It's actually a great step because your company matches a certain amount which is basically free money. You contribute three percent and they put another three percent in your account as well. Can't get a better return than that so easily in my opinion. Money in that account also grows tax deferred until it is withdrawn. This means you will have a lower tax bill at the end of the year which isn't too bad. And they have numerous funds pre-selected for the employees to choose from within the plan. Some of them track a specific index and some of them were mutual funds managed by fund managers. The index funds are usually cheaper and have passive management. Meaning the fund managers don't have to make too many decisions on buying and selling. It just tracks a sector or specific companies like large caps or publicly traded health care organizations. The actively managed mutual funds are the ones where the portfolio managers make more decisions and have a little freedom in choosing. Then there were a handful of target date funds that automatically adjust the closer you get to your selected retirement age.

"Which ones did we pick?" AJ asked.

We just picked a target date fund for you. I chose the year where you would reach age 67 and put 100% in there. That way you don't have to worry about constantly analyzing or rebalancing it yourself. Just set it and let the payroll deductions buy that same investment every two weeks.

"Do you do the same for your investments?" AJ inquired.

No. I use a few index funds such as a total domestic market, an international one, one real estate index, and one bond fund.

"Why do you use all of them?" Zoe asked.

There's a basket of companies in each one and it is much cheaper investing in all of them via the index. I just dollar cost average the purchases on a monthly basis.

"What's that?" Zoe probed.

Just basically investing a set amount on a specific date each month rather than all at once. Similar to how the 401k plan works where a designated amount is invested in your retirement plan on each pay date. I also have my own formula to determine how much is invested in each one of those vehicles as I get closer to retirement. Which may end up being the same retirement date you're targeting if college tuition doesn't start dropping.

"You're funny" Zoe said as she and her brother laughed.

But after you two learn a little more, we can switch from the target date to pick some index funds and I'll share my secret sauce. How's that?

"Sounds good Pop" AJ responded.

"I'll have some secret sauce of my own after I get my degree" Zoe said smiling and shaking her head yes.

I know you will. Better than mine I bet.

"Does God say anything about investing?" Zoe asked.

Well I believe He does. Do you remember the story about Joseph interpreting dreams for Pharaoh?

"I remember reading about it but not how it was related to investing" Zoe replied as she was looking up in the air trying to recall the actual story.

Remember when Joseph informed Pharaoh about his dream symbolizing an upcoming famine in the land.

"Yes" AJ replied as Zoe nodded her head in agreement.

Well prior to the seven years of famine were years of surplus. They were to gather some food to store at that time so it can be used during the famine. Well I'm teaching you to invest for very similar reasons. You need to invest in educating yourself, working hard and building assets early on in life so that you can use those investment returns while you're in retirement. They could also be used if you encounter any financially challenging times before then. Some people believe they'll be able to work forever or they'll somehow not run into problems along life's journey. We'll all have to stop or reduce our work load at some point. Either by choice or because our body forces us to do so.

"You're right dad. My body told me to retire every night I got home from my summer job" AJ added.

Your body is telling you to take some time for rest not full retirement young man.

"I know" AJ replied. "I cannot wait to finish school and grow my business to a billion dollar company so I can retire whenever I want. Then pass it on to however many children I'm blessed with."

That's a good point. Providing for your own and investing enough to leave an inheritance is also important. Even if you don't end up with a billion dollar business, just leaving a little is better than leaving them nothing at all. It will provide a great start. And if you teach them good money management skills, maybe they'll be able to grow the business and their personal finances more than we will accomplish. I want you two to be better than me in all areas. That's my goal and the reason why I share as much as I can.

"I pray all of my close friends are successful as well so we can enjoy taking trips together" Zoe said.

"Me too" AJ agreed. "I need a strong squad where we can talk about how all of our businesses are booming."

I share the same hope. Networking is very important and having a team around you with everyone managing money well magnifies the whole group. Make sure you follow your industry and attend relevant events so that you can meet people. Aim to always leave good first impressions, assist with serving them on projects or business ventures, and stay in contact. You never know who will be able to help you as you advance your career or your own company. I can remember at least two promotions due to great rapport I built with higher level staff members. It can only be beneficial.

"They can also help promote my business" AJ added.

This is true as well. Investing time into building a strong team is also great if you ever run into problems. If you are the only one in your circle who's doing well and you were to fall off, which one of your friends would be able to assist?

"Everybody may end up worst off in that scenario" AJ answered in agreement.

Exactly. But if each of you is successful, the others can provide a little help until you get back on track. None of them would have to give their all, but each one could depart with a little of their reserve until you're on your feet. They would be much more likely to do that collectively than taking a big hit separately. That's why it's great for your whole unit to be all-stars. People who aim to be the dominant MVP and not want anyone else to reach their level usually fall hard when they start to stumble.

"Uncle Cory says you're the MVP" Zoe replied grinning.

I'm sure he does… on days I agree to a loan.

CHAPTER VII: IT'S WORTH GIVING

It looks like the fish is just about ready. We'll leave it in for two more minutes. When they come out, you can add the last bit of glaze.

"Ok dad" Zoe replied.

AJ, please grab the spatula from the drawer and rinse it off.

"I'm on it" AJ responded.

Are you two ready for the community cleanup day tomorrow?

"Yes" Zoe replied. "I've been waiting to help Ms. Jackson with the garden."

I know you enjoy doing that.

"The work, not so much. But the results are great" Zoe clarified.

Well it takes a great amount of sowing to get a great result. If you all didn't put in that type of effort, she wouldn't be able to grow nearly as much.

"I agree" Zoe replied.

"My team is supposed to help with fixing up the playground" AJ said.

I know. I was just talking to Mr. Parrish about it last weekend. He was telling me how he received several big donations this year which will allow for the installation of a few new items.

"That'll be fun and I know the kids will enjoy it" AJ replied with a big smile on his face as he thought about how much he likes to build.

"I wonder who donated the most" AJ said.

Probably one of the Fortune 500 companies in the neighborhood.

"That's great that they do things like that" Zoe added.

It really is. Some of them do it for different reasons however. I would like to believe that most do it because the executives really care about the community. Then there are other companies that donate just for a tax write-off. Either way, it helps the recipient so I'm a proponent for anyone who wants to give back. Building up the community should be on the agenda for all residents whether it's where your home or business is located. Some may not have the financial means but volunteering time is also an important way to contribute.

"I'm definitely going to give back when my business is successful" AJ added.

You should. Any success is a blessing and part of the income gained should have a portion set aside to help others outside of just your family and friends. God says give and it shall be given back to you.

"Uncle Cory likes to say you give and you haveth no more" Zoe said before they all started laughing.

Uncle Cory is some character isn't he. There are plenty of others in the world that believe this as well. Mathematically if you give $10 out of your $100, you'll only end up with $90 for example. But God's math will have you with $90 initially before being blessed with much more. The more you help others, the more help you'll receive.

"Is that reaping what you sow?" Zoe asked.

It definitely falls under that principle. I also believe it falls under do unto others as you would have them do unto you. There may come a time when you're in need and would love if someone was able to help. Or maybe someone close to you is in need and you want to raise money for support.

"I think we should start our own nonprofit to help people" Zoe suggested.

That wouldn't be a bad idea. It takes a lot of work but it can be done. Start thinking about a specific mission that we can focus on and let's brainstorm on how to make it happen.

"I will" Zoe replied.

"Hey dad. Why do some people say they give and give? They tithe. They offer. But still seem like they're waiting for a breakthrough?" AJ asked.

"I had the same question" Zoe added. "Every Sunday morning when I turn on the television, I usually flip past a channel with someone preaching that this is the year for your breakthrough. I've heard that same line from the same people for at least three years" Zoe said as she shook her head.

"I bet next year will be the year as well. Especially if you send $49.49 within the next 49 minutes" AJ mocked before he and his sister burst into laughter.

Boy you've been hanging around your Uncle Cory too much. Well my opinion about that is God loves us too much to hurt us.

"Huh?" AJ responded baffled and having a hard time understanding how that related to not getting a breakthrough.

Do you two believe that I love you beyond measure?

"Of course" Zoe replied as AJ nodded in agreement.

How about when you were just starting elementary school?

"I think I was probably your favorite back then" AJ said smiling at his sister.

"Please. I've always been Daddy's angel" Zoe quickly countered.

Well you both were equally my favorites. And I tried to give you the world. One Christmas I recall AJ saying he wanted a car at age 5. So I asked him to show me which one the next time the car commercial comes on television. The next thing I know, we were staring at the screen looking at a brand new truck.

"I think I remember that" AJ said as they giggled.

Do you know why you didn't get that truck?

"I was too young" AJ replied.

Let's say you weren't mature enough to handle that type of gift. I think God feels the same way about some things we ask Him to give us. Even though we may be faithful tithers, give to the poor, volunteer our time, etc. we may not actually be mature enough to handle some of our requests. Being omniscient, He knows what that gift would lead to. So once we mature a little more spiritually, I think He would be willing to give us a few of those desires if not all. That is unless there's another reason why we shouldn't have them.

"That makes sense. I think I'm mature enough for that truck now" AJ said looking at his father while motioning his right hand and leaning back as if he was behind the steering wheel.

You do huh? Slouched back with one hand on the wheel?

"I'm just cruising" AJ said smiling still in his imagination.

Well make sure you cruise through the rest of this school year and bring home some exceptional grades. Then we can see if a gift like that fits the budget.

About five years from now that is.

"So you believe that once those same people become spiritually mature enough to handle a large monetary increase for example, God will give it to them?" Zoe questioned.

I really do. Particularly if they wouldn't use the money to do sinful things. And that increase can come in any form. They may get a promotion, win something, someone gives them a few dollars or helps lower an expense for instance. They may try to build a playground on their own and then all of a sudden extra funding arrives.

"Just like Mr. Parrish" Zoe replied.

Exactly. It could be a number of ways God answers that prayer request. And I know for a fact Mr. Parrish is a giver. He gives a lot of his time and love to the kids in the community.

"He probably wishes he had millions so he could do even more for them and himself" Zoe added.

Maybe. He seems very content to me. Prosperity isn't all about money. Having a good peace of mind, minimal stress, and enjoying what you do daily is prosperous as well. I think he likes that more than cash.

"He probably does. I always see him smiling" AJ stated.

I'm sure he does. But don't think he doesn't have money because he lives in that same community and drives an economy car. Plenty of people who worked for thirty or forty years and consistently contributed to retirement plans end up becoming millionaires. Some have an account that grows to eight or nine hundred thousand and then a house which is paid off by then. If that house is worth at least $200,000 for example, they're considered a millionaire assuming no other debts. It's not hard when you commit to following God and good financial principles.

"He seems like the type that saves a lot anyway" Zoe suggested.

I don't ask people about their personal finances unless they mention it voluntarily. But as long as I've known him, he's been very frugal and budgets well. I'm willing to believe his net worth is much higher than a lot of people you see driving through the neighborhood in their sports cars. And I like sports cars personally. Nothing wrong with it if it fits your budget and you've handled your priorities first.

"Like after tithing, saving, paying bills, and giving back?" Zoe asked.

Exactly what I mean.

"Dad, what do you mean by net worth?" AJ asked.

Well your net worth is financially defined as the difference between your assets and your liabilities. The assets are things you own such as your home, cars, and the money in your bank accounts. The liabilities are things such as any debt you may have. To get a rough idea just add up the value of your house, vehicles, stocks, retirement plans, and bank accounts. Then subtract any debts such as loans or delinquent bills. The result would be your net worth.

"So for me, I only have a little in the bank and my 401k plan. Thankfully I don't have any debt other than this cell phone bill I'll be paying off soon. I guess I'm poor, huh?" AJ replied before his sister giggled.

Well I wouldn't say poor because your father has something set aside for you as well. And you at least have a positive net worth all by yourself.

"Sometimes I see students in the stands counting a bunch of twenty dollar bills and saying they always have money" Zoe said as she was remembering a group of guys from the opposing team at their homecoming basketball game.

There are plenty of people who like to show off and don't understand the difference between having cash and a positive net worth. Sometimes you may hear someone say such and such always has a hundred dollars in his pocket. Or maybe even a thousand. But that same person may not have any assets other than a devaluing car which is not yet paid off. Then they could have credit card debt, passed due bills, pay day loans, student loan debt, etc. Do you really want to be like that?

"Not at all. I might be rich compared to them" AJ responded.

Comparatively you probably are. Or close to it since their net worth is in negative territory. They really do not have any money but just don't know it yet. I'm impressed by people who have a large net worth rather than a bunch of twenties and no other assets.

"Around tax time they really like to show off. Driving in their new cars, feeling themselves" Zoe said smiling.

"But a few months later you'll see the repo man driving in it" AJ added before they burst into laughter.

ENDING: DINNER TIME

Ok kids. Go set the table and wash your hands. I'll grab the salad, breadsticks, and see what we have to drink.

"Yes sir" AJ responded.

"Dad I'm glad you know a lot about personal finance" Zoe said.

I'm glad I do as well. Finance is so important to daily living and someone in every family should at least know enough to share best practices.

"It really is" AJ added. "Almost everything takes some amount of money. You need to pay bills, buy food, buy clothes, pay for school supplies..."

That's definitely the truth. Cash is an important tool to trade for products and services. It is my duty to make sure you two understand how to manage it well. I want to see you both successful in life and with whatever business ventures you may have. And when I finally get grandkids wayyyyy down the line, you need to continue sharing our secret sauce from generation to generation.

"We may also need to share this recipe" Zoe added. "This fish is delicious."

I'm glad you like it. It was pure teamwork as this was our first time making salmon this way.

"It definitely can't be our last" AJ replied before taking another bite.

"Maybe next time we can invite Uncle Cory so he can be a part of the discussion" Zoe said.

You know what. That is a good idea. But this time, you two will lead the conversation. He's heard it from me more than he might like. I've planted and planted. So now you can come along and water the seed.

"I can't wait to school him" AJ said shaking his head in a yes motion. "I now have a few comebacks for things he's been saying."

You sure do.

"Me too" Zoe replied.

Just make sure you two don't beat him up with it. Forced information is not better than loving persuasion. Keep that in mind.

"How should we spark the conversation?" Zoe asked.

Maybe you can talk about something you spent money on or a project you want to start. If he says anything with financial relevance you can begin there.

"He'll probably talk about how he's building an app to forward all bill collector calls to each other. Then they can decide who's getting paid and who's not" AJ replied as he and his sister burst into laughter while their father smiled shaking his head.

There is clearly something wrong with my brother.

The Recipe for Balsamic-Glazed Salmon

Ingredients:
6 salmon fillets (5 ounces each)
4 minced garlic cloves
1 tablespoon of white wine
1 tablespoon of honey
1/3 cup of balsamic vinegar
4 teaspoons of Dijon mustard
Salt and pepper
1 tablespoon of chopped oregano

Instructions:
1. Preheat oven to 400 degrees F. Line a baking sheet with aluminum foil, and spray with non-stick cooking spray.

2. Coat a small saucepan with non-stick cooking spray. Over medium heat, cook and stir the garlic until it is soft. This should take about 2-3 minutes. Mix in the white wine, honey, balsamic vinegar, and mustard. Then add some salt and pepper. Simmer uncovered for about 3 minutes or until slightly thickened.

3. Arrange the salmon fillets on a foil-lined baking sheet. Brush the fillets with balsamic glaze, and then sprinkle with some oregano.

4. Bake the fillets in a preheated oven for 10 to 15 minutes. It should be about done once the flesh shaves easily with a fork. Brush the fillets with the remaining balsamic sauce and season them with a little salt and pepper if desired.

ABOUT THE AUTHOR

Antoine C. Boyd is a business professional and finance enthusiast who has a strong passion for helping people become financially fit. Growing up in Baltimore's Latrobe Homes, he learned at an early age how a family can make a dollar and a prayer stretch into whatever necessities were needed. Despite not being taught personal finance in the schools he attended, budgeting came naturally to him as he consistently watched his family make ends meet. It was very difficult to understand how cash was used in everyday life but there were very few related lesson plans in the K-12 curriculums or at church. Even in college, those basic finance skills weren't a focus unless one majored in that particular subject. Truly understanding the importance of managing money and realizing there were limited resources available to the inner city communities is what prompted his desire to educate others.

Mr. Boyd has worked for large corporations and local nonprofits as a Management Accountant, Credit & Collections Lead, and as an independent consultant counseling individuals who may not be able to afford high-priced advisors. He also has volunteered at UMUC as a mentor to undergraduate students. His vision is to help individuals achieve their financial goals and increase their net worth regardless of their socioeconomic status.

Mr. Boyd's academic background includes graduating high school at the Baltimore Polytechnic Institute, getting a baccalaureate degree in Finance from the University of Maryland, and completing a Master's in Business Administration at Frostburg State University. He also attained a Certificate in Financial Management from UMUC, Six Sigma Lean Green Belt certification, and is a Certified Nonprofit Accounting Professional. In his free time, Mr. Boyd enjoys eating out with family and friends, watching business shows, and reading the latest finance headlines. He is also an avid bible reader, studying about the Author and Finisher of his faith.

Thank You!

I would like to thank everyone who purchased this book and gave me an opportunity to express my opinions about personal financial management. It is my belief that every believer has a ministry and this was one platform I've been allowed to share mine. My ultimate goal is to assist with the Word of God being placed back into the local government, school systems, and our neighborhoods by concentrating on one topic at a time. I envision this subject taught using the Heavenly Father's guidelines at faith-based schools, colleges, churches, or being given as a summer reading assignment.

If you are influential in any of those areas, I pray that you would share this literary work with the decision makers or assist with the marketing and promotion. Additionally, honest reviews on websites would be appreciated. I am eager to read your feedback. Be blessed...

Thanks again for the support.

www.ingramcontent.com/pod-product-compliance
Lightning Source LLC
Chambersburg PA
CBHW061159040426
42445CB00013B/1734